PRINCEW

Healing the Broken vows: Navigating Divorce in the Modern Age

First published by Lagang Princewill 2025

Copyright © 2025 by Princewill Lagang

All rights reserved. No part of this publication may be reproduced, stored or transmitted in any form or by any means, electronic, mechanical, photocopying, recording, scanning, or otherwise without written permission from the publisher. It is illegal to copy this book, post it to a website, or distribute it by any other means without permission.

Princewill Lagang asserts the moral right to be identified as the author of this work.

First edition

*This book was professionally typeset on Reedsy.
Find out more at reedsy.com*

Contents

1	Introduction	1
2	The Reality of Divorce	3
3	The Emotional Journey	5
4	The Legal Maze	7
5	Financial Implications	9
6	Co-Parenting with Compassion	11
7	Redefining Your Identity	13
8	The Role of Therapy and Support Groups	15
9	Overcoming Social Stigma	17
10	Dating After Divorce	19
11	Forgiveness and Letting Go	21
12	Embracing New Beginnings	23
13	Lessons from Divorce	25
14	Conclusion	27

1

Introduction

Divorce is a profound and challenging experience that often brings up a whirlwind of emotions—pain, uncertainty, and loss. However, while the end of a marriage can feel like the closing of a chapter, it also opens the door to personal growth and renewal. This book acknowledges the deep emotional impact of divorce and understands that it's not just the legal separation that people face, but the emotional journey that follows. It emphasizes that the process of healing is complex and can be a difficult road to navigate. By offering guidance and understanding, this guide aims to be a supportive companion through the various stages of divorce, from initial contemplation to rebuilding a future.

One of the primary goals of this book is to provide practical strategies and emotional tools that can help individuals manage the tumultuous journey of divorce. It emphasizes the importance of taking the time to process feelings and highlights the necessity of making informed decisions that align with one's values and long-term well-being. Whether it's dealing with the immediate emotional fallout or preparing for life as a single person again, this book offers clear steps to support individuals during each phase. Through these actionable steps, readers are encouraged to rebuild their lives in a healthier, more empowered way.

Ultimately, this book seeks to foster hope and healing during one of life's most challenging transitions. While it doesn't minimize the pain of divorce, it recognizes that there is always a possibility for growth and transformation in the aftermath. It aims to help individuals rediscover their strength and resilience, reminding them that they are not defined by the end of a relationship. With compassionate advice and practical tools, readers can look forward to a brighter future, equipped with the wisdom gained through their experiences. This guide is not just a book about divorce—it's a roadmap for reclaiming happiness, peace, and a renewed sense of purpose.

2

The Reality of Divorce

Chapter 1:

Divorce is an often-painful reality that many couples face, and understanding why marriages fail is a critical first step toward navigating this process. While every marriage is unique, common causes of divorce include communication breakdowns, infidelity, financial stress, and a lack of shared values or goals. Over time, couples may find themselves growing apart due to unresolved conflicts, unmet needs, or simply changing life circumstances. The emotional disconnect that arises can make it difficult to maintain the bond that once brought them together. This chapter helps individuals recognize the underlying issues that may have contributed to their marriage's dissolution, providing a foundation for acceptance and healing.

The chapter delves into the complexity of relationships, emphasizing that divorce is rarely the result of a single event but rather a culmination of ongoing struggles. It encourages readers to examine their own situations with clarity, not from a place of blame, but with an understanding of how both partners may have contributed to the end of the relationship. It's essential to acknowledge that even though divorce can bring pain, it also opens the door to personal growth and freedom from unhealthy dynamics. This section helps individuals gain insight into the realities of marital breakdown, laying the groundwork for the journey ahead.

It also explores the societal and cultural stigma surrounding divorce, especially in communities where separation is seen as taboo. Recognizing that divorce doesn't make someone a failure but rather a person who is seeking a healthier path is an important mental shift. The reality of divorce, as presented in this chapter, reframes the process not as a tragedy, but as an opportunity for transformation and self-discovery. The goal is to provide an honest, compassionate perspective on divorce, allowing individuals to come to terms with the decision in a constructive and empowering way.

3

The Emotional Journey

Chapter 2:

The emotional toll of divorce is profound, and this chapter focuses on the rollercoaster of emotions that often accompany the end of a marriage. Grief is one of the first emotions experienced, as individuals mourn not just the loss of a partner, but the end of a life they envisioned together. Anger often follows, stemming from feelings of betrayal or unfairness. These emotions can be overwhelming, leaving individuals feeling lost and consumed by negative thoughts. However, the journey doesn't stop there. This chapter emphasizes that the emotional process is neither linear nor predictable, and understanding this can help individuals give themselves permission to feel the full range of emotions as they heal.

Guilt is another powerful emotion that many people grapple with during a divorce, especially if they feel responsible for the dissolution of the relationship. This chapter explores how guilt can be a natural response but can also become a barrier to moving forward if it isn't processed healthily. The key message is that both partners contribute to the breakdown of a marriage, and while reflection is important, self-blame is counterproductive. Acceptance is the final emotional phase covered in this chapter, encouraging individuals to come to terms with their situation and find peace with their past decisions. By acknowledging and addressing these emotions, individuals can begin to embrace their personal healing journey.

The emotional journey, as described here, also emphasizes the importance of seeking support from trusted friends, family, or a therapist. Divorcing is an inherently isolating experience, and having a supportive network can make all the difference in how one copes with the emotional fallout. This chapter underscores the significance of self-compassion and encourages individuals to be patient with themselves as they work through the difficult feelings that arise. It is through this emotional healing process that individuals can eventually reach a place of acceptance and begin to rebuild their lives.

4

The Legal Maze

Chapter 3:

Navigating the legal aspects of divorce can feel like a complex and intimidating process. This chapter provides an overview of the legal maze that individuals must maneuver when seeking a divorce, starting with understanding the various grounds for divorce, such as irreconcilable differences, adultery, or abandonment. It highlights the importance of educating oneself about divorce laws in the specific jurisdiction, as legal requirements can vary widely depending on the region. Understanding what rights and responsibilities each party holds is crucial in ensuring a fair and informed divorce process.

This section also addresses the necessity of seeking competent legal advice to guide individuals through the intricacies of divorce proceedings. A skilled attorney can help navigate child custody arrangements, asset division, alimony, and other legal complexities. The chapter encourages individuals to take time to carefully consider their legal options and understand the potential outcomes of different decisions. Choosing the right attorney can make a significant difference in the process, as their expertise ensures that one's interests are properly represented.

Additionally, the chapter discusses alternative dispute resolution methods such as mediation and collaborative divorce, which can offer less adversarial and more cost-effective ways to handle divorce. It stresses the value of trying to resolve conflicts outside of the courtroom when possible, as litigation can be emotionally draining and expensive. Ultimately, this chapter provides a balanced approach to the legal aspects of divorce, emphasizing that while the process can be challenging, having the right legal support and understanding the necessary steps can lead to a more successful and fair outcome.

5

Financial Implications

Chapter 4:

One of the most daunting aspects of divorce is its financial implications, which are explored in this chapter. The process of dividing assets and debts can be contentious, especially when significant assets or investments are involved. The chapter emphasizes the importance of a clear and transparent assessment of financial holdings, including property, retirement accounts, and debts. Understanding how these assets will be divided based on state laws or pre-existing agreements is vital to avoid future conflicts. The emotional weight of financial insecurity or a sudden change in lifestyle after divorce is also acknowledged, providing a realistic perspective on the aftermath of such changes.

Alimony is another key financial topic covered in this chapter. Many individuals are unaware of how alimony is determined or how long it will last. The chapter explains the various factors that courts consider when awarding alimony, such as the length of the marriage, the standard of living, and each spouse's financial needs. By understanding these factors, individuals can better prepare for the financial consequences of their divorce. It also highlights the importance of updating financial plans, including budgeting and savings, in order to establish financial independence post-divorce.

Finally, the chapter encourages individuals to seek the assistance of financial advisors or divorce accountants who specialize in divorce settlements. These professionals can help create a comprehensive financial plan that addresses both short-term needs and long-term financial stability. Whether it's through negotiating property division or creating a post-divorce budget, expert advice can ease the burden and ensure that individuals are better prepared for their financial future. By taking proactive steps to manage the financial aspects of divorce, individuals can avoid some of the common pitfalls that lead to financial difficulties after the split.

6

Co-Parenting with Compassion

Chapter 5:

For individuals with children, co-parenting can be one of the most sensitive and challenging aspects of divorce. This chapter emphasizes the importance of putting the children's emotional and psychological well-being first. It highlights the need for parents to work together, despite their personal differences, to create a stable and supportive environment for their children. Effective co-parenting involves open communication, mutual respect, and a shared commitment to raising children in a positive and nurturing environment. Even though the parents may no longer be together, the chapter stresses that they must remain united in their parenting approach.

A central theme of this chapter is compassion—toward both the children and the ex-spouse. Children often experience emotional turmoil during a divorce, and it is essential for both parents to acknowledge this and offer consistent emotional support. The chapter suggests developing a parenting plan that includes clear expectations, visitation schedules, and a unified approach to discipline and major decisions. By focusing on compassion and cooperation, parents can minimize the negative impact of the divorce on their children and help them adjust more easily to their new family dynamic.

Additionally, the chapter addresses the importance of self-care for parents. Co-parenting can be emotionally exhausting, especially when dealing with unresolved conflicts or complicated family dynamics. The chapter encourages parents to take care of their own emotional health, which will ultimately benefit the children. It suggests finding support networks, including co-parenting classes or therapy, to help navigate the complexities of sharing parental responsibilities. By prioritizing compassion and cooperation, parents can create a healthy co-parenting arrangement that benefits everyone involved.

7

Redefining Your Identity

Chapter 6:

Divorce can be a transformative experience, particularly when it comes to redefining one's sense of self. This chapter explores how individuals can rebuild their identity after a marriage ends. The dissolution of a marriage often leads people to question who they are outside the context of being a partner or spouse. It's not uncommon for individuals to lose sight of their personal desires, dreams, and values during their marriage. This chapter encourages readers to reclaim their individuality and reconnect with their passions, interests, and goals. Rediscovering oneself is a vital part of the healing process and sets the foundation for moving forward.

The process of rebuilding self-esteem and self-worth is another key focus of this chapter. Divorce can significantly affect one's self-confidence, especially if the relationship involved emotional or physical abuse. The chapter provides strategies for rebuilding self-esteem, such as setting small goals, seeking therapy, and surrounding oneself with positive influences. It emphasizes that healing from a divorce involves not just letting go of the past but also embracing a new vision for the future. By redefining one's identity, individuals can find empowerment in their new chapter of life.

Finally, the chapter explores the idea of embracing new opportunities. Life after divorce can be a chance for personal growth, whether through pursuing a new career, traveling, or forming new relationships. It encourages individuals to let go of the fear of the unknown and embrace the possibilities that come with starting over. By focusing on self-discovery, self-compassion, and personal empowerment, individuals can move forward with confidence and a renewed sense of purpose. This chapter serves as a reminder that, while divorce may mark the end of one chapter, it also opens up a world of new beginnings.

8

The Role of Therapy and Support Groups

Chapter 7:

In the aftermath of a divorce, many individuals may feel isolated or unsure of how to move forward emotionally. Therapy plays a crucial role in helping individuals process their emotions, gain clarity, and learn healthier coping mechanisms. Professional therapists provide a neutral and safe space to explore feelings such as anger, sadness, or guilt. They help clients uncover any underlying issues that contributed to the dissolution of the marriage, allowing for personal growth and healing. Therapy is not just about processing emotions but also about building resilience and learning strategies for managing future challenges.

Support groups, on the other hand, offer a unique communal approach to healing. These groups allow individuals going through similar experiences to come together and share their stories. The sense of shared understanding in these spaces can be incredibly therapeutic, as it helps people feel less alone. Support groups also provide practical advice, coping strategies, and emotional validation, which can significantly boost a person's sense of empowerment. Being able to talk to others who have walked similar paths fosters a sense of hope and strength, enabling participants to realize that healing is not only possible but often a shared experience.

The combination of professional therapy and support groups creates a powerful toolkit for navigating the emotional rollercoaster of life after divorce. While therapy offers individualized, expert guidance, support groups create a sense of community that reinforces feelings of connection and solidarity. Embracing both forms of support helps individuals rebuild their emotional well-being, restore confidence in themselves, and pave the way for a healthier and more balanced future.

Overcoming Social Stigma

Chapter 8:

Divorce is often accompanied by societal judgment, and individuals may find themselves facing harsh opinions, especially in cultures that place a strong emphasis on marriage. The stigma surrounding divorce can lead to feelings of shame, guilt, and inadequacy. It may affect how individuals see themselves, often causing self-esteem to take a hit. The social expectations placed on divorced individuals can make them feel like they are viewed as failures or incapable of maintaining lasting relationships. Overcoming this stigma requires a shift in perspective, both from the individual and from society as a whole.

One key to overcoming social stigma is to redefine the narrative around divorce. Instead of seeing it as an end to a person's happiness or success, it can be viewed as a new beginning and a necessary step towards personal growth. Many individuals who have experienced divorce find that they learn valuable lessons about themselves, their needs, and their desires, which ultimately help them make healthier decisions in future relationships. Recognizing that divorce does not define who you are can help individuals reclaim their sense of identity and build a life that is fulfilling on their own terms, free from the judgment of others.

Another important aspect of overcoming stigma is self-compassion. It's essential for individuals to embrace their own journey, regardless of society's perception. By accepting that life is full of transitions and that every relationship has its unique story, individuals can begin to embrace their own process of healing. They can use their experience as an opportunity to educate others, challenge societal norms, and build a more supportive, empathetic community for people who have experienced divorce. The key lies in letting go of the fear of judgment and focusing on personal healing and growth.

10

Dating After Divorce

Chapter 9:

Re-entering the dating world after a divorce can feel daunting, but it can also be an empowering and transformative experience. For many, the idea of dating again brings up fears of vulnerability, rejection, or repeating past mistakes. It's essential to approach dating with a sense of self-awareness and clarity. Individuals need time to heal emotionally before jumping into a new relationship, as entering the dating scene while still healing can hinder both personal growth and the development of healthy new connections. Taking the time to rediscover one's identity, passions, and desires outside of the previous relationship is an important step toward dating with confidence.

When the time feels right, the process of dating after divorce should be approached with patience and open-mindedness. Building new connections doesn't mean rushing into a serious relationship but rather taking the opportunity to explore what one values in a partner and in a relationship. It's essential to enter new relationships from a place of emotional strength, knowing one's worth and boundaries. With a healthy mindset, dating can become an exciting avenue for growth and learning, offering the opportunity to meet new people and build connections that may align more closely with one's current needs and goals.

Confidence is key when dating after a divorce. Embracing vulnerability and openness allows individuals to form deeper, more meaningful connections. However, it's also important to recognize when things aren't right and to be willing to walk away if a relationship is not serving one's best interests. The lessons learned from past relationships can guide individuals in making healthier choices and cultivating more fulfilling relationships. Dating after divorce is a journey that can ultimately lead to greater self-discovery, healing, and the opportunity to build a future based on mutual respect, trust, and shared values.

11

Forgiveness and Letting Go

Chapter 10:

Divorce often brings a great deal of pain, not just from the end of the relationship but from the feelings of betrayal, anger, and hurt that may linger long after the separation. Forgiveness is a powerful tool in letting go of this emotional burden. It is not about excusing or forgetting the wrongs done but about releasing the hold that resentment and anger have over one's emotional well-being. Forgiveness allows individuals to reclaim their peace, no longer allowing past hurt to define their present or future. It is a process that requires time and patience, and it is ultimately an act of self-care and empowerment.

Letting go goes hand in hand with forgiveness. It is about releasing the attachment to past grievances and creating space for healing and growth. Holding onto grudges or lingering anger can impede personal progress and prevent individuals from moving forward with their lives. Letting go does not mean that one condones the actions that led to the divorce, but rather that they choose to stop carrying the emotional weight of those actions. This process involves accepting the past, learning from it, and making a conscious decision to live a life that is not dictated by bitterness.

The healing that comes from forgiveness and letting go is transformative. It allows individuals to cultivate emotional resilience and embrace a sense of freedom. By releasing negative emotions, individuals open themselves up to new possibilities, including healthier relationships, a renewed sense of self, and greater peace of mind. Forgiveness is a gift to oneself, freeing individuals from the shackles of past pain and enabling them to build a brighter, more fulfilling future.

12

Embracing New Beginnings

Chapter 11:

Divorce can mark the end of one chapter in life, but it can also signal the start of a new, exciting beginning. Embracing new beginnings requires a mindset shift—one that focuses on growth, possibility, and the excitement of creating a new life. Setting new goals is an essential part of this process. Whether it's embarking on a new career, learning new skills, or pursuing personal passions, setting clear intentions helps individuals redirect their energy towards building a future that aligns with their true desires. It is important to view this new beginning as an opportunity to shape a life that is authentic and fulfilling.

Change can be intimidating, but it is also an inherent part of personal growth.

After a divorce, individuals often find themselves in a position to redefine who they are and what they want from life. This process may involve stepping outside of one's comfort zone, exploring new interests, or even relocating to a new place. The key is to embrace change with an open heart and mind, understanding that it is through change that we often find the greatest opportunities for growth and fulfillment. Each new experience is a chance to create a life that is more in line with one's values and aspirations.

Building a fulfilling future after divorce requires resilience, optimism, and an unwavering commitment to self-improvement. Embracing new beginnings is not about forgetting the past, but rather using it as a springboard to create something better. By staying focused on personal growth, building supportive relationships, and remaining open to new experiences, individuals can create a future that is even more rewarding than the one they left behind. The journey of embracing new beginnings is one of empowerment, discovery, and the excitement of forging a path that is uniquely their own.

13

Lessons from Divorce

Chapter 12:

Divorce, while painful, can also serve as a powerful teacher. The experience of navigating through the end of a significant relationship often brings profound insights and valuable lessons. People learn about their own strengths and weaknesses, their needs in relationships, and their capacity for resilience. The emotional and practical challenges of divorce force individuals to confront their own vulnerabilities, but they also open up opportunities for deep self-reflection. This newfound wisdom can help individuals make wiser decisions in the future, not just in romantic relationships but in all areas of life.

One of the key lessons from divorce is the importance of self-awareness.

Going through the end of a marriage often leads to a deep exploration of one's values, desires, and emotional needs. Many individuals find that they develop a greater sense of self-worth and clarity about what they want in their lives and relationships. Divorce offers an opportunity to shed old patterns and beliefs that may have been holding them back, making way for healthier, more fulfilling connections. The lessons learned can also extend to improved communication skills, boundaries, and a greater understanding of what makes a relationship successful.

Ultimately, the experience of divorce can transform pain into wisdom. Individuals who approach their divorce with a mindset of growth and learning can use the experience to emerge stronger and more capable of creating the life they want. Rather than viewing divorce as a failure, it can be seen as an opportunity to gain valuable insights that will shape a brighter future. The lessons learned through divorce empower individuals to move forward with greater emotional intelligence, wisdom, and a clearer vision for the future.

14

Conclusion

In conclusion, divorce marks a pivotal moment in life—not merely as the conclusion of a relationship, but as the opening of a new chapter. The process is undoubtedly difficult, often laden with emotional, mental, and practical challenges. Yet, within these trials, there exists the potential for profound personal growth and self-discovery. Divorce provides a unique opportunity to reexamine your life, reassess your goals, and reconnect with who you truly are, free from the constraints of a partnership that no longer serves you.

The tools and insights shared in this book are not just about coping with the immediate pain but about equipping you with the resources to heal and emerge stronger. As you move through this journey, it's important to remember that healing is not linear, and growth comes with its own pace. There may be moments of doubt and setbacks, but the encouragement here serves to remind you that these struggles are part of the transformation. Through self-care, reflection, and persistence, you can begin to create a future that reflects your true desires and aspirations.

Ultimately, this book emphasizes that you are not walking this path alone. Divorce can feel isolating, but it's important to acknowledge the countless others who have navigated these waters before you, and those who will walk beside you. The future is filled with endless possibilities—many of which are waiting for you to embrace them. As you step forward, empowered by the lessons learned, trust that the life you can build is brighter, more authentic, and more fulfilling than you ever imagined.